CONFIDENT

52 Reminders for consistent confidence
in the inconsistent world of sports

Christen Shefchunas

CONFIDENT
52 Reminders for Consistent Confidence
in the Inconsistent World of Sports

Author: Christen Shefchunas
Editor: Taylor Brien
Cover Design: Nicole Wurtele
Interior Layout: Michael Nicloy

ISBN: 979-8-9881891-9-0

PUBLISHED BY CG SPORTS PUBLISHING

AN IMPRINT OF
NICO 11 PUBLISHING & DESIGN
MUKWONAGO, WISCONSIN
MICHAEL NICLOY, PUBLISHER
www.nico11publishing.com
Quantity order requests can be emailed to:
mike@nico11publishing.com

Printed in The United States of America

"I would not be where I am today if I hadn't reached out to Christen. She helped me set myself up mentally to succeed despite the pressure and nerves that I was facing. She has helped me overcome so much in this sport, leading me to accomplish my biggest goals of being an Olympic Gold Medalist and setting a World Record. Working with Christen has totally changed my career and I'm going to do it as long as I swim."

Gretchen Walsh
Olympic Gold Medalist
and World Record Holder

INTRODUCTION

If you've been an athlete for a while, you know how inconsistent the world of sports is. One day, you're thriving. The next, you're in a slump.

That inconsistency can easily lead to struggling with confidence.

And when you're struggling with your confidence, it's easy to forget.

It's easy to forget what you're capable of doing.

Easy to forget all the work you've put in.

Easy to forget who you are.

It's easy to forget the truth.

To be consistently confident, you must remind yourself of the truth: You've done the work. You know who you are. You're more than capable.

This book contains some of the most important reminders I use to help my athlete clients.

You'll read many examples and stories from swimming, as most of my clients are swimmers. But no matter your sport, this book's short, powerful reminders will meet you where you're at in your journey to help you stay consistently confident in the very inconsistent world of sports.

1.

I was coaching a transfer swimmer who had been stuck for years. She was frustrated, disappointed, and sad. She was ready for a fresh start and had walked into a new chapter at her new university — and my program — full of hope. But unfortunately, the bad swims continued. And with every bad swim, she again lost hope and was ready to quit.

I tried talking to her, but she told me she was fine. It was obvious that she had no interest in getting honest about what was going on.

Then one day in a meeting, I asked her what she was thinking behind the blocks. (If you're a swimmer, you know that being behind the blocks can be one of the scariest places in the world because that's where you're feeling the pressure to perform.)

She closed her eyes, thought about it for a few seconds and said, "What if I lose? What if I don't go fast? What if I'm just not as good as I think I am?"

She was pretty shocked when those words came out of her mouth. She had been hiding that for a long time, and for the first time, she was not only being honest with me, she was getting honest with herself. It felt so freeing to talk it out, and as she talked about it more, a weight lifted off her shoulders. She was so relieved to finally say it.

She also found hope again — because when she finally admitted what was going on in her head, she was able to do something about it. And that freed her to get unstuck and finally perform at her potential.

In sports, you're taught that being mentally tough means being fearless. So you never want to admit that you have negative thoughts, doubts, or fears. Athletes fake it, hide it, and lie about it. And that leaves you in a place where you can't do anything about it. You can't do the work if you're not willing or able to be honest.

If you're lying, hiding, or faking it, confidence cannot live there.

REMINDER:

*Confidence always
revolves around truth.*

2.

I like to challenge my clients to be honest about what's going through their heads when they feel the pressure to perform. I tell them to create a list of their thoughts.

The lists often go like this:

What if I disappoint my coach, my parents, my team, or myself?

What if I embarrass myself?

What if I get beat or _____ beats me?

What if I'm out of my league or I don't belong here?

What if I don't get recruited or get to go to the school I want to go to?

What if I'm not ready? What if I'm not prepared?

What if I'm not good enough?

What if I don't get the cut? What if I add time?

And this is one I hear a lot from team-sport athletes:

"My first couple of plays will determine my confidence. If they're good, then I'm good. But what if I mess up or do something dumb? I will struggle with confidence for the entire game. So basically, going into a game, I get anxious because I feel like my performance is a toss-up."

If any of those thoughts sound familiar, know that you are 100% normal. If you think like this, it doesn't mean you're weak. It doesn't mean you can't be confident or mentally tough. There is nothing wrong with you.

Even the best in the world have similar thoughts.

I've challenged every one of my Olympic and national team clients to bring back a list of their scary thoughts of when they feel the pressure to perform. I've never had one of them not bring back a list — because this stuff is 100% normal.

REMINDER:

*"What ifs" can be scary, but they
are totally normal. They don't
mean you can't be confident.*

3.

Most athletes are taught that they can get confidence from their coaches.

This lesson not only leaves athletes dependent on coaches, but athletes are looking to coaches for something they can't give them.

Here's the truth: The only person who can build your confidence is you.

Coaches can validate you, and believe in you, and say nice things to you, but they can't give you confidence. It is on you to build your own confidence, and when you take that responsibility seriously, you will thrive.

REMINDER:

*Your confidence is
your responsibility.*

4.

"I'm a better practice swimmer."

I hear that from swimmers who work hard and go fast in practice but then can't do the same at competitions. They struggle mentally at competitions, which causes them to perform poorly, and they convince themselves they can't swim fast at meets.

Think about who you are in practice. You're willing to take risks. You're willing to lean into the pain and fight through it. You're willing to give it everything you have — because you're strong and powerful … and willing to fail.

But at competitions, you feel nervous, which leaves you feeling weaker. And because there's more at stake, you're not willing to take risks because you're too afraid to fail.

Think about who you are in practice. That's you. No one else does that work for you. No one else pushes through the pain for you. And no one else takes those risks for you.

The strong, powerful risk-taker in practice is the same athlete at competitions, even when you feel nervous.

REMINDER:

Remember who you are in practice. That's you, even when you feel nervous.

5

When you walk into a high-pressure moment and start to feel vulnerable, you might start looking for things to control.

You might think, *If I knew what was about to happen, I'd feel more in control of this situation.* And you start trying to predict how things are going to go. In your mind, you start going through all the possible scenarios.

But there are two big problems with trying to predict what's going to happen. First, you're not a psychic, and you don't own a crystal ball. You cannot predict the future.

Second, when you do try to predict how things are going to go, you almost always end up imagining worst-case scenarios. You start thinking about everything that could go wrong.

And when you start thinking about everything that could go wrong, you panic.

Panic will always hinder your performance. I've learned you can perform well when you're nervous and you can even perform well when you're scared. However, you cannot perform well when you're panicking.

REMINDER:

You do not own a crystal ball. Trying to predict the future often leads to panic.

6.

Have you been called an "overthinker"? I talk to athletes all the time who feel a lot of shame because they've been told that they overthink.

But overthinking is often just a way of trying to find control. Overthinking is your mind going through all the details and all the different scenarios of what might happen in the future — because then it feels like you have more control over an unknown situation.

But remember, you do not own a crystal ball. No matter how hard you try, you cannot predict the future. Overthinking does not give you more control.

You can waste time and energy going through all the details and scenarios of what might happen, or you can save some energy and get your mind into the present. Focus on what you know now.

REMINDER:

If you find yourself overthinking, get your mind out of the future and into the present.

7

An Olympic swimmer once told me that she had been taught to stand behind the blocks at a competition and recite positive affirmations:

"I will win today."

"I will go a best time today."

"I will get this cut today."

But there was always a problem for her because down deep, she didn't believe it.

We all have a down deep that always tells us the truth, whether we like it or not. And you cannot con yourself into believing something that you don't actually believe.

I'm sure there have been moments in your career when you are having an internal conversation with yourself, trying to get yourself to believe, *I got this*. But your down deep lets you know, *I'm not sure we've got this.*

Remember, confidence always revolves around truth. In the pressure moments, you can't con yourself. You have to fully believe what you're telling yourself.

REMINDER:

*Stop trying to con
yourself into believing
something that you don´t.
Speak the truth.*

8

What if I haven't done enough?

I frequently hear that fear from athletes when they're preparing for a competition — and I don't hear it from slackers.

I hear it from hard workers.

Most hard workers feel like they should always be doing more, which leaves them feeling like they've never done enough.

Here's the good news: Every time you show up and put in work, you are putting money in the bank. And you don't have to start a new bank account each season. You have one account, and money has been going into that account since you started your sport.

So, if you've been doing your sport for a while, you're a millionaire. Some of you are billionaires.

At a competition, it's important to think about all of the deposits you have in the bank. It's a great reminder that you have done enough to be prepared for that moment.

REMINDER:

*Every time you put in work,
you put money in your bank.
You're a millionaire.*

9.

Most athletes understand that to feel confident, you need to feel prepared.

Yet, so many athletes do 99 things right and one thing wrong in practice, and they leave practice only thinking about the one thing they did wrong. And they beat themselves up about it.

Serious question: How will you feel prepared if you only focus on the things you do wrong? And how do you feel confident when you're constantly beating yourself up?

To feel prepared, you have to start paying attention to the 99 things you're doing right and give yourself credit for them.

REMINDER:

*Give yourself credit for the 99
things you're doing right.*

10.

The sports world does a terrible disservice to athletes by teaching overdependence on coaches. From a young age, athletes are taught to go to their coach for everything: *Tell me what to do. Tell me what I need. Tell me how I feel. Motivate me. Validate me. Give me confidence.*

It's easy to become dependent on coaches for everything, and in turn, athletes don't learn to trust themselves.

I know college swimmers who ask their coaches for a warm-up at competitions. They've been swimming for more than 10 years, and they don't know what to do for warm-up? Of course, they do! But they don't trust themselves because they've always depended on their coach.

These same athletes go to their coaches before races, hoping they can get some confidence from them. They are completely dependent on someone else for their confidence.

No one knows you better than you know you.

No one knows your body better than you know your body.

No one can give you confidence — that's your responsibility.

Stop depending on others to tell you what you already know. Stop depending on others to give you things you can give yourself. You can't bet on yourself if you don't trust yourself.

> ## REMINDER:
> *The more independent you are as an athlete, the more you will trust yourself. The more you trust yourself, the more powerful you will be.*

A client went to a competition and did well in all of her events. She swam best times in every event, and she was really happy with the meet.

But a week later, one of her rivals went to another competition, and she did well.

The next week when I talked to my client, all she could do was talk about her rival and how well she had done.

I said, "Good for her, but let's get back to you. I want you to walk me through each day and each event, and tell me how you did at your meet."

She did that, and when she was done, she was pretty stunned and said, "Thank you for making me do that. I had almost forgotten how well I had done."

"Yes," I said. "Because the minute you compared yourself to your rival, it was as if she took those great swims away from you. Did she? Of course not, but that's how comparing feels. It feels like someone is taking something away from you."

This is why comparing can be so dangerous. It leaves you feeling like you're not doing enough, and you're not good enough.

Never allow comparing to take your "yay!" away.

My client said "yay!" after her competition, but once she compared herself to her rival, the "yay!" went away. In her eyes, what she did was no longer good enough.

Most athletes will find themselves comparing themselves to rivals at some point. It's a pretty natural thing. But you have to get good at catching yourself and remind yourself, *No one is taking anything away from me*.

It's your responsibility to focus on you, your journey, and your "yays!"

REMINDER:

Never allow comparing to take your "yay!" away.

12.

You cannot control your competitors. You cannot control your teammates. You cannot control what others are thinking. You cannot control what comes out of your coaches' mouths or their decisions. You cannot control the clock.

So. What *can* you control?

It's simple:

Showing up and giving 100%. That's it.

I tell swimmers, there are no jetpacks that you can throw on to go faster in that moment. The only thing you can do is show up and give 100%.

The good news is that that's something you know how to do. You do that every day in practice. You're actually really good at that.

When you're feeling overwhelmed, ask yourself, *What can I control?* That question not only simplifies things and puts the focus on you and what you can control, it also gets you into the present.

REMINDER:

*The only things you can control
are showing up and giving 100%.
You know how to do that.*

13

When I talk to Olympians, I'm always blown away by the amount of failure in their journeys. We only see the highlight reels of their career.

I often hear that those failures got them to where they are now because they learned things they wouldn't have learned if everything had gone right.

Failure is an inevitable part of sports, and it is hard. It hurts, and it's embarrassing. And because it's so hard, it's common to try to move forward fast and pretend everything is fine.

But if you take the time to process failure and be honest with yourself, you can learn so much about yourself, your training, your mental game and how you can be better.

- Look at yourself. It's easy to blame others when things don't go right. Take the time to look at yourself and be honest with yourself. What do you need to change? What could you have done better? Did you struggle mentally?

- Communicate with your coach, and talk about the training. What worked? What didn't work? Is there anything that needs to be changed in the future?

- And here's one few people think about: What new fears will start to show up because of this failure? (FYI, *What if it happens again?* will be one of them.) You'll want to do the work and be as prepared as possible for when those show up in the future.

REMINDER:

Failure is an inevitable part of sports. Take the time to learn from it.

14.

Most athletes are taught that "mentally tough" means, no matter what, suck it up, put your head down, and just keep pushing.

So that's what you do if you have fears, doubts, and negative thoughts at competitions.

If you're dealing with depression or your mental health: *Suck it up, put your head down, and just keep pushing.*

If you're not sure you believe in yourself anymore because you've been struggling: *Suck it up, put your head down, and just keep pushing.*

If life is pretty tough outside of your sport: *Suck it up, put your head down, and just keep pushing.*

But there are major problems with this way of thinking.

Just because you put your head down doesn't mean those struggles aren't there. These are the things that hold you back from reaching your potential, and you've been taught to pretend that they're not there. You've been taught to run away from reality.

You've been taught that being mentally tough means running away.

But in truth, being mentally tough is having the courage to be honest with yourself. And, great news! When you're honest with yourself, you can do something to help yourself.

It's time to redefine "mentally tough." It's not faking, pretending or running away from reality. It's having the courage to say, *Yep, I'm going to be honest about this AND I'm going to do something about it — because I'm not going to allow this to hold me back from what I know I'm capable of doing.*

REMINDER:

Mentally tough is NOT sucking it up and pretending you're fine. Mentally tough is having the courage to be honest with yourself so you can help yourself.

15

I was working with a swimmer trying to make her second Olympics.

To feel more in control, she was thinking through all the scenarios that might happen at Olympic Trials. I told her that she was wasting energy. She wouldn't know the outcome until she touched the wall at the end of her race and looked at the scoreboard.

She didn't like what I had to say and had a mini temper tantrum. "But I want to know what's going to happen!" she said. "I want to know! I want to know!"

I understood. If she knew what was going to happen, it would take a lot of pressure off her shoulders. But there was a problem: She was not a psychic nor owned a crystal ball.

I told her that she had two options. She could continue to have a temper tantrum, or she could accept that she cannot predict the future.

She needed to get out of the future and stop making up stories about what *might* happen. She needed to focus on the present and what she knew right then.

At Olympic Trials, she didn't have a temper tantrum. She chose to focus on the present and what she knew. And she made her second Olympic team.

REMINDER:

*You cannot predict the future,
and it's time to accept that.*

16.

A great way to get yourself into the present when you're nervous is to ask yourself, *What do I know now?* And then answer it.

A client wanted to be prepared to answer that question when she felt nervous. So she created a list the night before her competition:

What do I know now?

I know exactly how to swim this. I've swum it a million times

I know I am the same swimmer as the one in practice who is strong, powerful, and focused. I never give up, and I fight through pain, no matter what.

I know I'm a billionaire.

I know I have no control over anyone else, and they have no control over me.

I know I did 20x200's last week in practice and this is 1x200. I can do 1x200.

She also wrote a dollar sign on her foot with a marker, so when she was on the blocks and looked down to take her mark, that was the last thing she saw before she dove in. That was her last-second reminder that she had a lot of money in the bank, and she was prepared for this moment.

Doing the work the night before gave her confidence that she was prepared to get present when she was feeling the pressure.

REMINDER:

To get your mind present,
answer the question,
What do I know now?

17

A college golfer would go into a tournament expecting perfection, and when a hole didn't go as planned, she would panic.

Things would go downhill quickly after that because no one can play well panicked.

The golfer knew she had to let go of perfection, so she chose a reminder that she would repeat to herself.

When things didn't go as planned, she would tell herself, *It doesn't have to be perfect to be good.* She could make a mistake or miss a shot and still have a great game. That reminder kept her from panicking, and it helped her stay calm and play her best, even when things didn't go perfectly.

REMINDER:

*It doesn´t have to be
perfect to be good.*

18

I was working with a basketball player who would stay after practice every day for an extra 20-30 minutes to work on her shooting.

Whenever I tried to validate her and tell her "good job" for that, her response was, "Not a big deal, that's just me. That's just what I do."

"No, that's not just you," I replied. "That's hard work. It's dedication. It's sacrifice. It's a choice."

I've learned that most hard-working athletes do a bad job of giving themselves credit. When you're a hard worker, and you're surrounded by other hard workers, hard work becomes normalized.

But hard work is a choice. You can choose to be a slacker, but you don't. You choose to be a hard worker. Your choices always deserve credit.

REMINDER:

Putting in hard work is not "just you." It's a choice. Your choices deserve credit.

19.

I hate to break it to you, but you are not going to be great every day. I have never met an athlete who doesn't have days when everything seems harder than usual.

If you've been doing your sport for a while, you know that some days, you go in and give your best, and it's pretty impressive. But other days, you give your best and it is ugly.

This is a reality that every athlete in the world experiences.

Give yourself some grace. Stop beating yourself up. Give yourself credit for giving your best.

REMINDER:

Your best is going to look different on different days.

20

I challenge all of my clients to start a confidence journal. The idea behind the journal is that every day after practice, they will write down at least one thing that they did well.

I start with just one thing because most athletes are only focused on the one thing they're doing wrong, instead of the 99 things they're doing right.

When they commit to finding at least one thing they do well at practice, they start looking for the good stuff. All of a sudden, instead of being able to write only one thing, they can write a few things.

After a couple of weeks or months of writing, they will be able to go back to this journal before competitions and see concrete proof of all the hard work they've put in.

If you think a confidence journal could be helpful for you, look at it as part of your training. Just like you wouldn't miss a day of physical training, don't miss a day of mental training.

When you commit to writing in this journal consistently, it does three important things.

1. It is your responsibility to remind yourself of the truth. This journal will be full of reminders of the truth, and the more you write in it, the more reminders you will have.

2. When you make a goal to write in it every day, and you stick to it, you will feel accomplished. Any time you feel accomplished, you build your confidence.

3. You will walk into future competitions knowing, *I not only stayed consistent with the physical training, I stayed consistent with the mental training, too.* That's a level of confidence very few athletes have.

REMINDER:

Be consistent with your confidence journal.

21.

It's important to add mental wins to your confidence journal, too.

When you show up to practice, and you are not in the mood, but you pull yourself together and give 100%, that should be in your journal because that will be a reminder that you know how to get yourself into a better place mentally, even when you start from a negative place.

When you're in a practice that's not going well, and you are frustrated, but you pull yourself together and finish strong, that should be in your journal because that's going to be a reminder that you know how to get yourself into a better place mentally, even when you're frustrated.

And when you are more focused on your teammates because they are beating you that day, and you're angry, but you put your focus back on yourself and what you can control, that should be in your journal, too, because it will be a reminder that you know how to get your focus back to you.

When you walk into a competition and worry that you might struggle mentally, these will all be reminders of the truth: You know how to get yourself into a better place mentally.

REMINDER:

Journal your mental wins, too.

22

You are not going to feel motivated every day.

Even when you're very serious about your sport and passionate about getting better, you will still have days when you will struggle with motivation.

When motivation isn't there, that's when you have to choose to be disciplined.

Here's the truth: If you want to do great things in your sport, you cannot wait around to feel motivated. You have to choose to be disciplined.

REMINDER:

Choose to be disciplined on days when you don´t feel motivated.

23

You're not always going to feel ready. And that's OK! Because being ready is not a feeling. It's a choice.

The choice is: *Are you willing or not?*

Are you willing to show up and give 100% — even when you don't know what's going to happen?

Are you willing to lean into the uncomfortable?

Are you willing to take that risk?

Are you willing to lean into fatigue and pain?

Sometimes being ready is as easy as being willing.

REMINDER:

Being ready is not a feeling.
It's a choice.

24

I worked with an Olympian who had no life outside of her sport. Her whole world revolved around her sport. If she had a bad practice or a bad competition, it was like the world was ending. She would go home and think about it nonstop and beat herself up over it.

She knew this wasn't working, and she had to make some changes. She needed to give herself some grace and understand that her best would look different on different days. But she also desperately needed to find some balance in her life.

I asked her what she liked to do outside of sport, and she had a hard time answering. She looked back at her childhood and said that she used to enjoy puzzles. So I challenged her to buy a puzzle and do it after practice. It would give her something to think about other than her sport.

She ended up loving it! It was fun, and it gave her mind a break from thinking about her sport.

Seeing the difference that little change made in her life, she started trying new things and created a life for herself outside of her sport.

She learned that she didn't have to think about her sport 24/7 to be great at it. Finding some balance not only made her happier and healthier, it made her a better athlete, too.

REMINDER:

You don´t have to think about your sport 24/7 to be great at your sport.

25.

If you walk into a competition thinking, *I have to win, I have to go this time, I have to perform well,* you are adding a lot of pressure onto yourself. That pressure is heavy, and it will hold you back from your potential.

I call it the "heaviness of the have-tos."

It is your responsibility to be aware if you are walking into a competition with a "have-to." And it is your responsibility to get that "have-to" off your shoulders. The only thing you *have to* do is show up and give 100%. That's the only thing you can control, anyway.

REMINDER:

*Get those heavy "have-to's"
off of your shoulders.*

26.

Too many athletes panic after a bad practice.

They panic because they think a bad practice means something. They fear it defines their future. They go into worst-case-scenario thinking: *This bad practice means I'm not going to be good at the next competition. This means I'm a bad athlete. This means I'm going to have a terrible season....*

Here's the truth: Bad practices are inevitable in sports. No athlete in the world is great every day.

After a bad practice, it is your responsibility to remind yourself that a bad practice does not define your future, and a bad practice does not mean you're suddenly a bad athlete. This is all part of the process, and there is no need to panic.

REMINDER:

The better you handle the inevitable bad practices, the sooner you will bounce back.

27.

I once worked with a tennis player who felt anxious before matches and after he made mistakes.

During one of our calls, I asked him, "Is there anything that could come at you on the court that you wouldn't know how to handle?"

He thought about it and realized his answer was "no." He knew exactly what he was doing.

A few months later, he was at a big tournament, and he was sending me nervous texts before his matches, all the way up until the quarterfinals. Then, he went silent.

Afterward, I got a text that said, *I won. I started to get really nervous, but then I REMINDED myself: This is what I do. Being nervous doesn't suddenly mean that I don't know how to play tennis. Of course, I know exactly what I'm doing.*

Though that sounds so basic, it's a truth that he knew deep down.

You've raced your race and played your game so many times. Reminding yourself that you know exactly what you're doing, even when you're nervous, can be very powerful.

REMINDER:

This is what you do. You know exactly what you´re doing, even when you´re nervous.

28

A game-changing moment for an Olympian was when she finally understood that if she felt a lot of pressure, she would end up with negative thoughts, fears, and doubts. She finally accepted that she was going to go there — but she just couldn't stay there.

Before this, when she had doubts, she'd worry that something was wrong. She'd worry that she wasn't mentally tough enough, and she'd fear that going into a negative place meant that she wouldn't perform well.

And she panicked, which held her back from her potential.

When she accepted that she was going to go there and normalized some negative thoughts showing up, she stopped panicking. And when she stopped panicking, she was able to get herself into a better place mentally.

REMINDER:

Normalize the nerves.

29

When you want to feel more in control, you will start to predict. And when you start to predict, you often end up imagining worst-case scenarios.

Unfortunately, a lot of athletes will then start to prepare themselves for that worst-case scenario, and they start to self-sabotage. For example, an athlete might think, *If I don't do well, I still have more chances in the future* or *It's OK if this doesn't go well.*

If you think that way, you've prepared yourself for a made-up story that you're going to fail.

And when you start preparing yourself for failure, you panic.

Stop preparing yourself for a made up story. Instead, catch yourself if you're in a worst case scenario and bring your focus back into the present and what you know now.

REMINDER:

Don't self-sabotage by preparing yourself for a made-up story in your head.

30

Ever notice how your mind doesn't like staying present, especially when you're nervous?

Your mind wants to go into the past and remind you of your bad performances and failures, which makes you doubt that you can succeed. Or it wants to jump into the future and predict more bad performances and worst-case scenarios, which brings a dread that you're going to fail again.

Your brain loves the past and the future when you're nervous. It does not love the present.

You cannot just hope that your mind will be present in a pressure moment. It is always an intentional decision to pull your mind into the present and focus on what you know *now*.

Being in the present not only helps you be calmer before competitions. The present is where you can perform at your fullest potential.

I often hear people say, "Stay present." But there's no staying present when you're nervous. It's all about *getting* present. And that is your responsibility.

REMINDER:

*Getting present is always an
intentional decision.*

31.

A lot of athletes expect to show up to their competitions feeling perfect. No pain, no soreness, no fatigue.

But you are rarely going to feel perfect at competitions. I hear all the time, "I don't feel good in the water" or "My legs feel really tired," and the athletes start panicking.

Good news! You don't have to feel perfect to be good.

Think about how many practices you've gone through when you didn't feel perfect. You still showed up. You still fought, and I bet a lot of those practices went a lot better than you thought they would.

Stop panicking if you feel sore or tired. You can perform well when you don't feel perfect.

REMINDER:

*You don´t have to feel
perfect to perform well.*

32.

As a competitor, frustration is inevitable.

It's hard to watch other people do better. It's hard to watch other people go faster. It's hard to watch other people achieve goals you haven't — yet.

But it's called a "comparison trap" for a reason.

When you are more focused on others than on yourself, you live in frustration.

Living in frustration will always leave you trapped.

You can be frustrated, but you don't need to live there.

When you find yourself comparing, it is your responsibility to put your focus back on yourself and what you can control.

Because here's the truth: You have no control over how others do. You have no control over how fast others go.

The only thing you can control is continuing to show up and taking steps toward your goals. When you get your focus back to you, you can move forward and not get trapped.

And remember, just because someone gets to a goal before you do does not mean that yours isn't coming. And it doesn't mean that your success isn't going to surpass theirs.

Don't give up hope just because someone gets there before you. We all get there at different times.

REMINDER:

Don't get caught in the comparison trap. Get your focus off of others and back to yourself.

33

I was talking to an athlete who felt like she had had a great practice, but no one had told her, "Good job."

Not a coach. Not a teammate. No one.

And because she didn't get validation from anyone, she wondered, *Maybe it wasn't as good as I thought.*

In that moment, she talked herself out of giving herself credit for that great practice, because in her mind, the practice wasn't good unless she heard "good job" from her coach. She was dependent on others to validate her.

Validation feels good. It's nice to know when others notice the good stuff you're doing. But the most powerful athletes don't need validation from others because they already know they're doing a good job.

When you give yourself credit consistently, external validation becomes less important.

You can still want the validation, but if you don't get it, you must learn to validate yourself and give yourself credit for the steps you're taking and the choices you're making.

REMINDER:

Validate yourself.

34.

I was working with a swimmer who was feeling anxious before her races. I asked her what she does before her races, and she told me that she likes to visualize her race.

I asked her for more details, and she told me that she visualizes herself swimming her race, and then she sees herself win the race.

I told her that some athletes feel extra pressure by visualizing themselves winning. I asked her why she visualized it that way, and she told me a successful athlete who did it that way told her to do it, too. So she started doing it but never paid attention to whether it was helping or hurting her.

When she took the time to figure out what worked for her, she realized that she still likes to visualize, but she doesn't like to "see" any other swimmers in the pool. She focuses on herself.

Visualizing this way, she felt less anxious before her races.

There are a lot of tips out there for athletes. And a lot of them are great. But you should realize that not every tip or every piece of advice will work for you. Try it, but pay attention: Is it helping you or hurting you?

REMINDER:

*Pay attention to what works
and what doesn't work for you.*

35

I was working with a Division I lacrosse player whose greatest fear was losing her starting job.

She lost it, anyway.

Then, coming off the bench, she played better than ever.

I asked her what changed, and she said she was playing more like herself. She was taking more shots. She was being more aggressive. She was playing with courage.

I asked her why she didn't play that way when she was a starter. As she talked it out, she realized that she wasn't willing to take risks when she was starting. She was playing it safe.

She was playing to not lose her starting job.

She didn't take shots because she was too afraid to miss them. She didn't play aggressively because she was too afraid to make a mistake. Her fear of getting benched kept her from taking risks.

But by not taking those risks, she wasn't playing like herself. She wasn't playing at her potential.

Here's the truth: To be your best, risks are required.

REMINDER:

*You'll never know how good
you can be if you're not
willing to take risks.*

36.

Many athletes expect to show up to their pressure moments fearless and in a perfect mental state. Then, the minute a fear or doubt shows up, they panic.

Here's the truth: It doesn't have to be perfect to be good.

You can have some fears and doubts and still be in a good place mentally.

Your thoughts can feel messy, and you can still be in a good place mentally.

You can have some freakouts and still be in a good place mentally.

REMINDER:

*You don´t have to be in
a perfect place mentally
to be in a good place.*

37.

A bad competition does not define your future, but how you react to it can.

When athletes have a bad competition, panic comes easy. They imagine worst-case scenarios and worry that they're not good anymore — and that they are stuck there forever.

Then, they take that panic into their next competition. Panic holds them back from competing well, the panic grows, and the cycle continues. This is how athletes get stuck.

Bad competitions are an inevitable part of sports. They are normal. Competing poorly does not mean that you're suddenly a bad athlete, or that this is where you will be stuck forever.

It is your responsibility to stay calm, stay focused, and stay in the process.

REMINDER:

*Don't panic after
a bad competition.*

38.

I have learned that the more you want it (want to win, be great, etc.), the more stubborn you will be. And the more stubborn you are, the more you will want to control things you cannot control.

Being stubborn isn't all bad. It keeps you determined, striving, and moving forward. But it can hold you back in a big way, because being stubborn leads you to try to control things you cannot control, including other people. And you have zero control over other people.

If you've ever been called stubborn, be aware that you probably try really hard to control things you cannot control. Your job is to get your mind back to you and what you can control.

REMINDER:

*The more stubborn you are, the more you will want to control things you cannot control.
Get your focus back to you.*

39.

I was working with a young woman who had a very legitimate chance of making the Olympic team. But on our last call before Olympic Trials, we didn't spend time talking about how she could be in the best place mentally.

She was in an unhealthy relationship, and we talked about how to protect herself from any drama that her boyfriend may start while she was at Trials.

We spent more time talking about how to create boundaries without upsetting him than we did about her success.

As you can imagine, Olympic Trials did not go well for her.

Show me your friends (or boyfriend or girlfriend), and I'll show you your future.

You are responsible for surrounding yourself with people who support you, cheer for you, and who will never try to sabotage your success.

And it is your responsibility to walk away from anyone who brings toxicity, drama, and pain into your life.

You have too much potential to let someone else's drama get in the way of your success.

REMINDER:

It is your responsibility to surround yourself with the right people and walk away from others.

40

I worked with an elite athlete who was very confident, but she was not performing at her best in her highest moments.

As we talked, I realized that she was desperate to be in a good place mentally, so when fears and doubts showed up, she'd try to block them out.

"I just try not to think about them," she told me.

I hear that from a lot of athletes — "I'm just going to try not to think about it."

But my response is, "You do know that if you're trying not to think about it, that means that you're already thinking about it? So how about you admit that you are thinking about it, so you can actually *do* something about it?"

REMINDER:

If you're trying not to think about it, you're already thinking about it. Admit it, so you can do something about it.

41

When I was a college coach, I learned to give my athletes mental health days. I understood that the grind of sports is real. It's easy for life to feel like an exhausting rotation of eating, sleeping, schoolwork, and sport. It can deplete you mentally.

If my athletes needed a practice off, they just had to send a text: *mental health day*. They didn't need to tell me why. They didn't need to give me details. I trusted that they knew themselves better than anyone, and if they needed to take a practice off for their mental health, I encouraged it.

Some would use it to take a nap. Others would catch up on their schoolwork, talk to their therapist, or maybe get a massage. I knew doing these things would be so much more helpful than coming to another practice and getting even more mentally depleted.

The next day at practice, I always saw that they could breathe easier. They made a decision that was best for them. They protected their mental health, which is always the right decision.

REMINDER:

Your mental health must always be your priority.

42

I was working with a very stubborn Olympic athlete. Every time I challenged her to try something new, her response was, "I'll try, but it's hard."

Finally, after hearing that response several times, I called her out. I said, "Yes, it is hard. But you know how to do hard! You do it every day. And you do it really well."

Sports are hard. Training is hard. Pressure is hard. Getting into a good place mentally is hard. Good news! You know how to do hard things. You do it every day.

REMINDER:

You know how to do hard.

43.

Most swimmers put a lot of pressure on themselves in their first event. In their eyes, if their first race goes well, the entire meet should go well. But if the first race doesn't go well, it's going to be a bad meet.

The question I get the most from swimmers is, "How can I move forward after a bad first race? How do I not panic?"

You can do only two things in this situation: First, learn from it. Ask yourself, *What can I do better next time?*

Second, find some perspective.

How many times have you started a practice and it wasn't going well, but then something clicked, you found your groove, and you started crushing it? I guarantee it's happened plenty of times.

How many times have you had a horrible morning practice, but that evening's is your best practice of the week? I guarantee that's happened plenty of times, too.

And how many times have you had a horrible practice one day, but the next day, you feel like a new person? Yep, that's happened a lot, too.

One race does not define the entire competition.

REMINDER:

You can always come back from a disappointing start.

44

When you're feeling the pressure, it's easy to forget who you are.

I worked with a field hockey player who played well in lower-pressure games. But when faced with better teams, she felt nervous, struggled with confidence and did not play well.

I asked her if she knew why she wasn't playing well, and she said, "That's easy. I don't play like myself. I don't play like me."

So I asked her what it looks like to play like herself. "Give me some words," I told her, "that define who you are when you're playing like yourself."

She said:

"I'm confident."

"I'm fast and strong."

"I'm fiery."

"I'm tactical."

"I'm composed."

"Wow!" I said. "That sounds like a really good field hockey player." She agreed.

She decided to write those words on her field hockey stick, so when she was in the higher pressure moments and felt nervous, she had a reminder of the truth about who she is directly in front of her.

REMINDER:

*Consistently remind
yourself of who you are.*

45.

"What if I'm in a good place mentally, and then I just lose control?"

"What if I get in my head, and I cannot get out?"

I get those questions all the time, and my response is: "Remember, we are talking about *your* mind. It's yours. How do you lose control over something that is yours?"

Now don't get me wrong. You do not have control over your mind wandering. Your mind loves wandering out into the future to try to figure out what's going to happen. It probably seems like your mind loves going into the chaos.

But you do have control to catch yourself when you are in the chaos and say, *No! I'm not going to stay here*. You have control to bring yourself into the present and focus on yourself and what you can control.

A swimmer kept a Post-it on her mirror all season that said "I'm in control" because she'd feel pretty good mentally until about 20 seconds before she heard, "Step up on the blocks." Then, she would feel out of control and panic.

When she started to remind herself that she was, in fact, in control, she was able to catch herself, get into the present and focus on herself, which allowed her to reach her full potential.

REMINDER:

*You will get nervous,
but you can control it.*

46

Some days you got it. Some days you don't.

I hear that from athletes all the time, and I'm sure it's happened to you. There are some days when you feel pretty confident and some when you feel you have no confidence at all.

Athletes will say, "I went into that competition with absolutely no confidence."

I get it!

But I don't buy it.

Confidence is like the sun. Even though you can't always see or feel the sun because clouds might be covering it, that doesn't mean it's not there.

Confidence is the same way. It's always there, but the clouds are fears, doubts, mistakes or bad races. However, just because the clouds are there and you can't feel your confidence, it is still there.

What a great reminder as you're walking into a competition feeling as if you have no confidence — *Just because I cannot feel it doesn't mean it's not there.*

Remind yourself of some of your more confident moments. That is your confidence.

Own it at all times!

REMINDER:

*Your confidence is always there,
even when you can't feel it.*

47.

Let's talk about being positive.

Many athletes look at positivity like a light switch. They try to go from grumpy, negative, and nervous to "Yay! I'm so positive and happy, and life is full of rainbows and cotton candy!"

I wish it were that easy, but that is not realistic. Flipping the switch leads to faking it, and confidence always revolves around truth.

A college athlete I worked with was struggling with motivation at a competition. She went to her coaches and they told her, "Just be positive."

She tried hard to flip the switch and be positive, but it didn't work. She called me and explained that she had been studying for midterms and was tired and worn out. She just couldn't find any positivity.

I said to her, "Let me guess. You'd rather be in bed watching Netflix?"

"I'd love to be in bed watching Netflix!" she said.

You're allowed to feel that way, I told her. "But here's a truth I know about you," I said. "You're not the type of woman who ever walks into a competition and doesn't give 100%, right?"

"I would never not give 100%," she agreed. "But I'm allowed to not want to be here?" she asked.

"Of course you are," I told her. "The truth is, you're exhausted and worn down. You can be real about that. But here's also your reality: You are at a competition. And you're not the type of woman to give mediocre effort."

She was relieved to know that she could be real about her feelings. But she also embraced her reality and remembered who she is. She is someone who always shows up and gives her best, even when she doesn't feel positive.

REMINDER:

You can be real about your feelings and still be positive.

48.

The night before a big competition, a swimmer sent me the mental work she had done for it.

On the left side of a piece of paper, she wrote out all of her fears and doubts that she knew would show up the next day. From each, she drew a little arrow to the right side of the paper, where she wrote the reminder that she will need when that fear shows up.

A few examples from her work:

What if I don't go my goal time —> I don't have a crystal ball. Focus on executing the race well. I'll know my time when I touch the wall and look up.

What if I lose —> I don't have any control over anyone else. I will get my focus back to me and what I can control, which is showing up to these blocks and giving 100%.

What if I'm tired —> How many practices have I been tired, and I still showed up and had a great practice? It's happened so many times in my career. I can swim fast [while] tired.

What if I'm not prepared —> I'm a billionaire. I have so much money in the bank.

By doing the work, she was not only prepared to handle those fears, but she walked in with confidence, knowing that she was physically *and* mentally prepared.

REMINDER:

Before competitions, do the work to mentally prepare yourself.

49

As high-pressure competitions approach, life can feel more stressful, and you can become more sensitive and fragile. It is your responsibility to take care of yourself well. Part of taking care of yourself is protecting your peace.

A few tips:

- Take a step back from anyone or anything that could bring drama or negativity into your life.

- Allow yourself to get more rest. Now is the time to be a little boring.

- Delete or mute any social media that could trigger you or put you in a bad place mentally.

- Distract yourself. Listen to some podcasts. Binge-watch some shows. Do your homework. Keep your mind occupied by things other than your sport.

- Write out your thoughts to clear your mind when you're feeling overwhelmed.
- Prioritize sleep.
- Be kind to yourself — no beating yourself up.
- Be honest with yourself. Face your fears courageously.

REMINDER:

*It is your responsibility
to protect your peace.*

50.

You have no control over anyone else.

That's easy to say. It's a little harder to accept.

When you finally accept that truth, it might feel like a bit of power has been taken away from you. (Of course, that's not the case — because you never had any control over others in the first place.)

But that's how it feels.

Want to feel like you have a little power back? Remind yourself that no one has any control over you, either.

REMINDER:

You have no control over anyone else. Good news — they have no control over you, either.

51.

A reality check:

You are not going to be motivated every day.

You are sometimes going to dread going to practice.

You are not going to "trust the process" every day.

Sometimes, finding your "why" will be hard.

You will have a love/hate relationship with your sport.

You will get frustrated with your sport and sometimes wonder if life would be better without it.

You are going to cry over your sport.

You are going to struggle, lose, and be stressed and disappointed sometimes.

There is nothing wrong with you.

Perfect athletes don't exist. Perfect careers don't exist.

REMINDER:

*Stop beating yourself up
for not being perfect.*

52

Most athletes focus only on the physical work.

When an athlete has been stuck for a while, I often hear about the changes that they've made physically. They've changed their training, their nutrition, their weight program, their sleep routine, but they rarely have thought about their confidence or mental game.

And when they finally do the work, they realize that the mental work was the missing piece of the puzzle.

Here's the truth: Confidence takes work. Consistent work.

Commit to doing the work.

Journal daily.

Do the mental work the night before competitions.

Write down or talk things out when your thoughts become overwhelming.

Be honest with yourself.
Remind yourself of the truth.

REMINDER:

Confidence takes work.
Do the work.

Christen Shefchunas is a Professional Confidence Coach who works with World Record Holders, Olympians, and NCAA Champions. She is a former All-American Swimmer at the University of Tennessee and coached for 16 years, spending time as an assistant coach at Michigan State and SMU, and Head Coach at the University of Miami.

During her time as a coach, Christen watched too many athletes miss out on their potential because of their lack of confidence. Realizing that there was a significant lack of resources for these athletes, Christen left her coaching career and started Coach Christen, a business focused on helping athletes handle the pressure and build their confidence.

She works one-on-one as a confidence coach with some of the best athletes in the world and she is a sought after speaker, speaking to teams, athletes, coaches, parents, and business leaders about how to handle the pressure and how to build consistent confidence in the inconsistent world of sports.

www.ingramcontent.com/pod-product-compliance
Lightning Source LLC
Chambersburg PA
CBHW060533130626
46553CB00002B/735